STORIES FROM ANCIENT GREECE & ROME

by

Joyce Tyldesley

Illustrated by

Julian Heath

Published in the United Kingdom in 2017 by
OXBOW BOOKS
The Old Music Hall, 106–108 Cowley Road, Oxford OX4 1JE

and in the United States by
OXBOW BOOKS
1950 Lawrence Road, Havertown, PA 19083

Paperback Edition: ISBN 978-1-78570-765-0
Digital Edition: ISBN 978-1-78570-766-7 (epub)

For a complete list of Oxbow titles, please contact:

United Kingdom
Oxbow Books
Telephone: (01865) 241249
Email: oxbow@oxbowbooks.com
www.oxbowbooks.com

United States of America
Oxbow Books
Telephone: (800) 791-9354, Fax: (610) 853-9146
Email: queries@casemateacademic.com
www.casemateacademic.com/oxbow

Oxbow Books is part of the Casemate Group

CONTENTS

THIS BOOK BELONGS TO

The people of ancient Greece spoke the Greek language, but their version of the Greek language was not the same as the Greek language that is spoken in Greece today. If a modern Greek person travelled back in time to meet met an ancient Greek person, they would not be able to understand each other.

The ancient Greeks wrote their language using the ancient Greek alphabet. Can you write your own name in ancient Greek, in the scroll above? Not all of our letters occur in the Greek alphabet: they did not have the sounds J, Q, V and Y, so I have suggested some alternative letters for you. Remember to use the capital letter at the start of your name.

THE GREEK ALPHABET

	Normal letter	Capital letter			Normal letter	Capital letter
A	α	A		**N**	ν	N
B	β	B		**O**	ο	O
C	χ	X		**P**	π	Π
D	δ	Δ		**Q**	κ	K
E	ε	E		**R**	ρ	P
F	φ	Φ		**S**	σ	Σ
G	γ	Γ		**T**	τ	T
H	ʹ	ʹ		**U**	υ	Y
I	ι	I		**V**	φ	Φ
J	ι	I		**W**	ω	Ω
K	κ	K		**X**	ξ	Ξ
L	λ	Λ		**Y**	ι	I
M	μ	M		**Z**	ς	Z

The people of ancient Rome did not write their numbers in the same way that we do. They used letters to represent the numbers. We call these letter-numbers **Roman numerals**. We sometimes use Roman numerals today; you may have seen them on a clock or watch face. Can you write your own age in the scroll, using Roman numerals?

MY AGE

ROMAN NUMERALS

1	I	6	VI	11	XI	50	L
2	II	7	VII	12	XII	100	C
3	III	8	VIII	20	XX	500	D
4	IV	9	IX	30	XXX	1000	M
5	V	10	X	40	XL		

ABOUT THIS BOOK

When I was a schoolgirl (a very long time ago; I am **LVII** years old!), I loved to read the stories told in ancient Greece and Rome. I think that you will love reading these stories too. So in this book I have collected together ten of the most exciting tales, and I have asked my friend Julian to draw pictures of the stories for you. You might want to colour these pictures in.

One of the stories, **Romulus Builds a City**, comes from ancient Rome. The other nine stories are slightly older; they are stories that were told in ancient Greece. All the stories are fiction – this means that they have been made up. Some are stories that the people told to explain the things that puzzled them. Why are there different seasons every year? Why do bad things happen to good people? And why do all spiders create a web? But most are stories that were told simply for fun.

Happy reading!

Ιοιχε

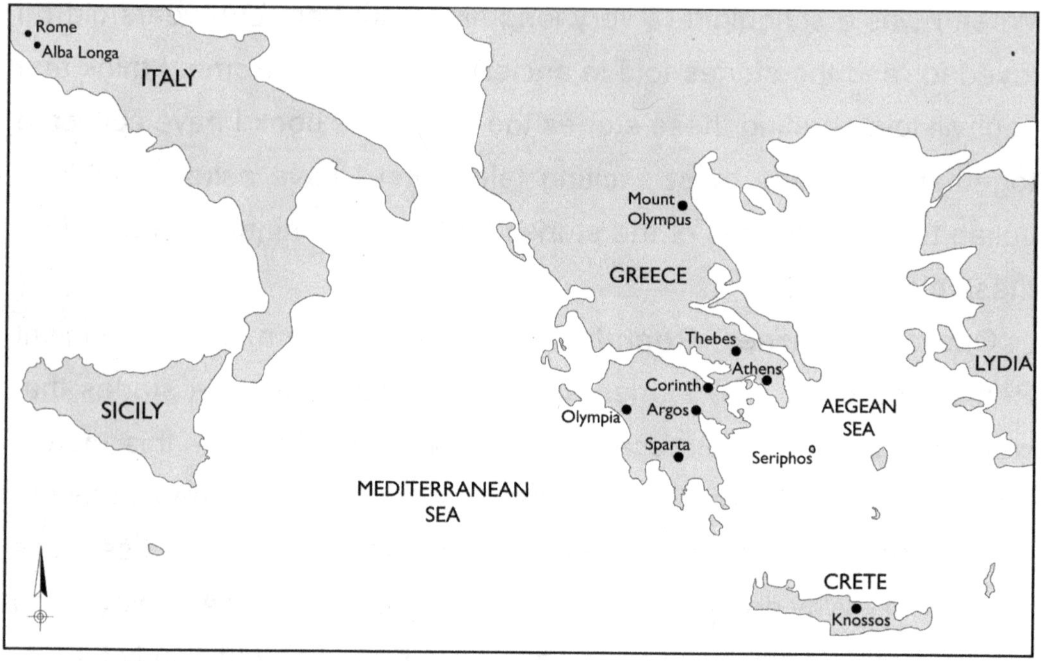

Rome
Alba Longa

ITALY

Mount
Olympus

GREECE

Thebes

Athens

Corinth

Argos

Olympia

Sparta

Seriphos

AEGEAN
SEA

LYDIA

SICILY

MEDITERRANEAN
SEA

CRETE

Knossos

This is a map of ancient Greece and Rome.

ABOUT ANCIENT GREECE AND ROME

Greece is a southern European country with a long coastline and thousands of islands scattered around the mainland in the Mediterranean Sea. Many hundreds of years ago, this land and its islands were divided into many small kingdoms or city-states. The people who lived in these city-states all spoke the ancient Greek language and all worshipped the same gods and goddesses, but each city-state had its own king and its own laws. Sometimes the city-states were friendly towards each other, and sometimes they fought fiercely against each other. The largest city-states were called Athens, Sparta, Thebes and Corinth.

The ancient Romans lived slightly later than the ancient Greeks, in the European country that we now call Italy. They worshipped the same gods and goddesses as the Greeks and told many of the same stories about them. However, they gave the gods and goddesses different names. So, Zeus the king of the gods in ancient Greece, was known as Jupiter the king of the gods in ancient Rome. The wise Greek goddess Athena became the wise Roman Minerva, and Aphrodite the ancient Greek goddess of love, was known as Venus in Rome.

1

PERSEPHONE VISITS
THE UNDERWORLD

The goddess Demeter worked very hard every day. It was her job to make sure that the people of Greece always had enough food to eat. She made the crops grow in the fields, the fruit ripen on the trees and the flowers bloom in the gardens. She taught the farmers how to plough the fields, and how to scatter seeds on the land. When the grain and the vegetables and the fruit had grown, she taught the farmers how to collect the plentiful harvest, and how to store it safely in their barns. Thanks to Demeter's hard work, the people of Greece never went hungry.

Demeter had just one child: a beautiful daughter, named Persephone. Persephone was as good and kind and cheerful as she was beautiful. She was a happy girl, who loved to sing and play in the warm sunlight while her mother was busy helping the people to grow their food. Everyone loved Persephone, but Demeter loved her most of all.

One sunny day, Persephone was singing and picking pretty flowers in the green meadow when Hades drove by in a golden chariot pulled by four fierce black horses. Instantly, Hades fell head over heels in love with the beautiful Persephone. He wanted her to be his wife, and to live with him forever. But Hades was no ordinary man. He was the god-king of the Underworld; the dark and cold land where the dead live as ghosts. The sun never shone in the Underworld. There were no green meadows, and no pretty flowers to pick. Hades knew that Demeter would never allow him to marry Persephone and take her to live in the gloomy Underworld, away from the warmth and sunlight that she loved. And so he decided not to tell Demeter what he was going to do. He simply reached down and dragged Persephone, kicking and screaming, into his chariot. Ignoring the girl's terrified screams, Hades drove as fast as he could away from the green meadow.

Persephone was very frightened. She cried and shouted for her mother, but Hades would not listen and would not stop. The four fierce black horses galloped as hard as they could, pulling the golden chariot for many miles, until they reached a broad and fast-flowing river. This river was home to a water spirit, or Naiad. The Naiad knew Demeter, and wanted to help Persephone. She made the river-water waters rise up and block the road. Finally, the golden chariot was forced to stop. This made Hades very angry. He struck the river with his stick and, instantly, the waters parted. A deep, dark crack opened in front of his golden chariot. Hades cracked his whip, and the four fierce black

horses pulled the golden chariot through the deep, dark crack, into the Underworld. Persephone just had time to untie her belt and throw it to the ground before the earth closed around her.

Hades and Persephone were married that day. Persephone was now the queen of the gloomy Underworld. She sat on a golden throne beside her new husband, and cried for the sunshine and flowers that she loved. Hades, who loved Persephone very much, tried to tempt her to eat with delicious cakes and fruits, but she would not stop crying and she would not eat anything. She did not hate Hades, because he was very kind to her. But Persephone did not want to live in the gloomy Underworld with the ghosts. She wanted to live in the warmth and sunlight, with her mother.

Returning home from work, Demeter found Persephone gone. Frantic, she started to search for her beloved daughter. The search went on for many days and, as she wandered the land, Demeter forgot her duties. The crops started to fail in the fields, the flowers began to rot in the gardens, and the fruit died on the trees. There was no food for the farmers to harvest. Soon all of Greece was hungry, but Demeter ignored the cries of the people as she continued to search for her lost daughter.

Eventually Demeter found Persephone's belt lying beside the river, and recognised it. Here, at last, was a clue. Demeter summoned the

Naiad who lived in the river, and asked if she had seen Persephone drop her belt. The Naiad was able to tell Demeter what had happened; how Persephone had been snatched by Hades and taken unwillingly into the Underworld to be his queen. Horrified by this story, Demeter appealed to Zeus, king of the gods, for help. She wanted her beloved daughter to be returned safe to her. She did not want her to live forever in the gloomy Underworld.

Zeus could see that Demeter would not stop grieving until she knew that Persephone was safe. It worried him that Demeter had abandoned her work, and that the people now had no food to eat. This situation could not continue. So he told Demeter to cheer up. Persephone was safe and fairly happy in the Underworld with Hades as her husband. Demeter, however, was not satisfied with this, and she begged Zeus to allow Persephone to return home to her mother. Zeus thought about the problem, then gave his judgement. Persephone could indeed return to her mother. However, there was one important condition. Persephone could only return home if she had not eaten anything in the Underworld. Filled with joy, Demeter sent a messenger to the Underworld to tell Persephone the good news.

When she heard her mother's message, Persephone burst into tears. Only that morning, feeling faint with hunger, she had eaten six seeds from a pomegranate fruit. Was she now doomed to live forever

in the gloom of the Underworld, because of six very small pomegranate seeds?

Demeter again turned to Zeus for help. Was her daughter really trapped in the Underworld because she had eaten just six very small pomegranate seeds? Again, Zeus thought about the problem, and gave his judgement. As she had eaten six seeds, Persephone was to spend six months of each year with her husband Hades, in the gloomy Underworld. The other six months of the year could be spent with her mother, Demeter, in the sunlit land of the living.

And this is exactly what happened. For half the year Persephone lived in the gloomy Underworld with her husband Hades. During these months Demeter abandoned her work and mourned her lost daughter. Without Demeter to care for them the crops in the fields slowly died, the flowers in the gardens withered, and the leaves and fruit fell off the trees. For the other half of the year Persephone left her husband in the Underworld and went to live with her mother. During these months Demeter, who was now filled with happiness, went back to work. She caused the crops to grow again in the fields, the fruit to ripen on the trees and the flowers to bloom once more in the gardens. Every year there was a plentiful harvest. Greece was once again a land rich in food, and the people were no longer hungry.

ABOUT PERSEPHONE'S STORY

The ancient Greek farmers had noticed that the year could be divided into four seasons: spring, when the leaves started to appear on the trees; summer, when the sun shone bright and hot; autumn, when the fruit was ripe on the trees; and winter, when the days were short and cold and nothing grew in the fields.

The story of Demeter and Persephone explained why this happened. Spring was the time when Demeter was looking forward to her daughter's return from the Underworld. Summer was the time when Demeter was happy because Persephone was with her. Autumn was the time when Demeter started to feel sad because Persephone would soon be returning to her husband Hades. And winter was the time when Persephone lived with her husband in the Underworld.

WHAT DO YOU THINK?

1. Why did the people love Demeter?

2. What does a pomegranate look like?

3. Do you know how many months there are in each year? And how many days there are in each month?

4. What foods do you think the ancient Greeks ate?

2

PANDORA OPENS A BOX

Many, many years ago, there lived two brothers named Prometheus and Epimetheus. The brothers lived at a time when only the gods and goddesses knew how to make fire. Prometheus, who was a brave and clever man, felt that this was very unfair. The gods and goddesses should share the secret of fire with the people. Prometheus travelled to Mount Olympus, the home of the gods and goddesses, and stole the secret of fire. He gave fire to the people. The people were now very happy; they could use the fire keep warm in winter, and could light lamps that would allow them to see when night fell. They could cook their food, and could melt metal to make useful tools. The gods and goddesses, however, were very unhappy. Zeus, king of the gods, was especially angry with the two brothers, and plotted his revenge.

Zeus asked the gods and goddesses to help him create a beautiful woman. The woman was modelled from clay and water, and given the gifts of beauty and grace. The gods and goddesses dressed her in lovely clothes and expensive jewellery, and taught her how to sew and

weave cloth. The beautiful woman was named Pandora. Pandora was almost perfect. She had just one fault: she was a very nosy person. She wanted to know absolutely everything about the all the people and all the things around her.

Zeus introduced Pandora to the two brothers. Knowing that he had annoyed Zeus, and worried that Pandora might be a trap, Prometheus refused to have anything to do with her. Epimetheus, however, took one look at the beautiful woman and fell in love. He decided that he wanted to marry Pandora. Although Prometheus warned him to be very careful, Epimetheus could not believe that a woman as beautiful as Pandora could be dangerous.

Epimetheus married the beautiful Pandora and they lived together in a pretty house surrounded by gardens and olive groves. Their world was a very happy place. Sadness, anger and worry did not exist, and there was no illness and no death. The people were cheerful and content; every day they sang and laughed and danced in the bright sunlight. Epimetheus and Pandora were the happiest of all the people, because they were very much in love.

Zeus gave Pandora and Epimetheus a beautifully carved wooden box as a wedding present. As he handed the box over, he gave them strict instructions that they should never, ever, under any circumstances open the lid and look inside. Epimetheus put the box in the corner of their bedroom, and forgot all about it. He was not a curious man. Pandora, however, was always curious, and she was fascinated by the beautifully carved box. Every day she wasted many hours thinking about it and looking at it. She really, really wanted to know what was inside the box in her bedroom. Could it be filled with expensive jewellery? Or with fine clothes that she could wear? Or maybe the box held an interesting book that she could read?

One day, as she stared at her carved box, Pandora was astonished to hear whispering voices coming from inside.

"Pandora, let us out. Please Pandora; we are trapped in here. Let us out to play with you."

Pandora could not bear not knowing what was living inside the carved box that Zeus had given her as a wedding present. Trembling slightly, she stretched out her arm to raise the lid. She had decided to take just one quick peep inside the box, without anyone knowing. At that very moment, her husband Epimetheus entered the bedroom. Seeing what Pandora was about to do, he shouted a warning:

"Pandora, stop! Don't do that. Remember, Zeus told us not to open the carved box under any circumstances. There might be something really dangerous trapped inside."

But his warning came too late. The curious Pandora had lifted the lid. A flock of strange creatures with sharp claws and jagged teeth and flew

22

straight at Epimetheus and Pandora. Ouch! The ugly creatures stung, and they scratched, and they bit, then they flew away, escaping through the bedroom window. Epimetheus and Pandora ran to the window and looked out. They could see the creatures stinging, and scratching, and biting their neighbours, and they could hear their neighbours crying in pain as the creatures flew by them.

Quickly, Epimetheus slammed the lid back down. For the first time ever, he was angry with the beautiful Pandora. They started their first quarrel:

"Why did you open the box, you silly woman? Do you not remember what Zeus said? That box was not to be opened under any circumstances. Zeus is the king of the gods. You should not have ignored his orders."

"You wanted to know what was inside just as much as I did, you stupid man. You should have stopped me from opening the box. You should have stopped the creatures from flying out. It is all your fault that they escaped. Now what are we going to do?"

Just then, they heard another, very small voice coming from the box.

"Pandora, please let me out. You have freed all the sorrows that were trapped in this box, and have allowed them to fly out into the world. Now for the first time, the people will feel sadness and anger and worry. They will argue and fight; they will grow ill and will eventually die. Let me out too, so that I many help the people to feel better."

Astonished, Pandora lifted the lid again. Squashed in the bottom of the box, she saw a tiny butterfly-like creature with delicate wings and a kind face. The tiny creature spoke again:

"My name is Hope. I cannot re-capture the sorrows that were trapped in this box, and I cannot stop them hurting the people. But I can help the people when they have been affected by the sorrows."

Hope flew out of the box, brushing Epimetheus and Pandora gently with his soft wings. Immediately they started to feel less angry, and more content. Hope then flew through the window, to help the people who were having to deal with sorrow in their lives for the very first time.

ABOUT PANDORA'S STORY

Modern science helps us to understand how the world works. Like us, the ancient Greeks wanted to understand how the world worked, but they did not have the scientific knowledge that we have. So they told stories to explain things that were very difficult to understand. This story explains why bad things, such as pain, war and illness, can happen to good people. The story starts in the very happy time when there are no sorrows in the world. No one gets angry or upset or ill, and no one dies. But Pandora's curiosity causes her to disobey Zeus's orders, and she opens the box. Her disobedience allows the sorrows to escape into the world. The sorrows cannot be re-captured, but Hope, who was also trapped in the box, allows the people to feel slightly better about their lives.

Pandora's story has been told for many hundreds of years, and is still being told today. It has changed slightly over time as it has passed from storyteller to storyteller. In the earliest versions of the story Zeus gave Pandora a big pottery jar known as a pithos, rather than a box. However, when the story was translated from the ancient Greek language, a mistake was made and the jar became a box. Grown-ups today still talk about a "Pandora's box" when they want to describe a source of unexpected troubles or problems.

WHAT DO YOU THINK?

1. Where do the gods and goddesses live?

2. Who is Zeus?

3. Why do you think that the people wanted the secret of fire?

4. Why did Pandora open the box?

3

THESEUS ESCAPES FROM THE LABYRINTH

King Minos ruled the island of Crete. He was a powerful and wealthy king who lived in a splendid palace and commanded, a large army and a big fleet of ships. But he was not a popular king because he was cruel and a bully. His people did not like him, and his neighbours were all frightened of him. They obeyed his orders and gave him many generous gifts because they were worried that he might attack their ships and invade their lands. The people of the kingdom of Athens were particularly frightened of Minos and his fierce soldiers and sailors. They did everything that he asked, quickly, because they were too frightened to say "no".

Minos lived in a splendid palace on the island of Crete with his wife Queen Pasiphaë and his daughter, Princess Ariadne. The palace had many beautifully painted rooms, every one decorated with precious rugs and expensive furniture. Wide windows filled the palace with light and fresh air, and allowed Minos to watch his fleet of ships sailing on the blue Mediterranean Sea. Every day the palace servants prepared

enormous banquets of delicious food and drink, while musicians and dancers and storytellers and acrobats entertained Minos and his family.

But there was another, hidden part of the palace that was not at all nice. Deep beneath the light and airy rooms there was a dark and damp dungeon. A thick wooden door in the dungeon wall opened into to a confusing maze of twisting and branching tunnels known as the Labyrinth. And at the heart of the Labyrinth there lived a fierce creature known as the Minotaur. The Minotaur looked like no other living being. He had the body of a man, but the head and sharp horns of a bull. The Minotaur was large and strong and always angry. He snorted and roared instead of speaking, and he pawed the ground with his large, hairy feet. His favourite food was human flesh. He was not fussy; he would eat babies and old people and even the occasional soldier who accidentally wandered into his Labyrinth. But he particularly liked to eat young men and young women. King Minos fed his Minotaur on young men and young woman from the kingdom of Athens.

Every year Minos ordered the king of Athens to send seven young men and seven young women on a ship to Crete. Because he was frightened of King Minos, the king of Athens always did as he was told. Fourteen young men and women said goodbye to their families, boarded a ship with black sails, and made the long, sad journey across the Mediterranean Sea. Minos would welcome the young people to his palace, introduce them to his family, feed them a splendid meal, then lock them in his dark and damp dungeon. There was no escape. Fourteen times the thick wooden door in the dungeon wall would be opened. Fourteen times a young man or young woman would be sent into the labyrinth. Here they would wander about, hopelessly lost and confused, until the Minotaur tracked them down and ate them. This situation made Aegeus, the king of Athens, very angry. But he knew that if he did not obey his orders, Minos would send his fleet of ships to destroy Athens, and many hundreds of people would die. And so, every year the ship with black sails made its sad journey across the Mediterranean Sea to Crete.

One day Prince Theseus, the son of Aegeus, king of Athens, asked his father why this sad journey must happen. Why should the people of Athens send seven young men and seven young women every year, to be killed and eaten by the Minotaur in the Labyrinth on the island of Crete? Aegeus sighed, wiped away a tear, and explained to his son that Minos was a powerful king whose soldiers and sailors could destroy Athens. The people of Athens dare not disobey his orders. If they did disobey, they might all die.

Theseus, who was a brave young man, did not agree with his father's decision to obey Minos's orders. He thought that it was time for the people of Athens to fight back against the bully from Crete. And so,

when the time came again to send seven young men and seven young women on the ship with black sails to Crete, he volunteered to be one of the seven young men. King Aegeus was horrified. He did not want his brave young son to be eaten by the Minotaur. But Theseus reassured his father: "Don't worry Dad, I will be fine. I am strong, and clever, and skilled at fighting. I will find my way through the Labyrinth. I will kill the Minotaur, and I will return to you on a ship with white sails. You will be able to see the white sails on my ship as you look across the sea, and you will know that I have succeeded in my mission, and that I am safe." Reluctantly, Aegeus agreed to Theseus's plan.

And so, when the time came, Theseus said a tearful goodbye to his family, boarded the ship with black sails, and journeyed across the Mediterranean Sea to the island of Crete. His companions, six worried young men and seven worried young women, hoped that brave Prince Theseus would be able to save them from the Minotaur, but they had no idea how he could do this. Theseus, too, was worried. He was determined to kill the Minotaur and rescue his companions, but as yet he did not have a plan.

The ship with black sails docked at the island of Crete, and the fourteen young people, Theseus included, were taken to the palace to meet King Minos, Queen Pasiphaë, and Princess Ariadne. They ate a splendid meal of meat, fish, vegetables and fruit, then the guards dragged them off to the dark and damp dungeon to await their fate.

Unlike her father, Princess Ariadne was a good person. She was also very clever. She knew that a fierce Minotaur lived in the Labyrinth under the palace, and she knew that this Minotaur liked to eat young men and women. Every year she saw seven young men and seven young women arrive from Athens and disappear into the palace dungeon, never to be seen again. This year, she had resolved to save the fourteen young Athenians if she could.

Late that night, when everyone was asleep, Ariadne crept to the palace dungeon and opened the door. She handed Theseus a gleaming sword and a large ball of wool. Theseus was confused. The sword would obviously help him to kill the Minotaur. But what was the large ball of wool for? Ariadne explained. After finding and killing the Minotaur, Theseus would need to find his way out of the twisting and branching tunnels of the Labyrinth. He could do this easily if he tied one end of the ball of wool to a nail in the Labyrinth doorpost, and unwound it as he made his way through the tunnels. Once the Minotaur was dead, he could follow the wool trail back to the dungeon door. The Athenians could then escape from the palace and run to their ship in the harbour. Theseus thought that this was a brilliant plan. There was just one problem:

"Will your father, King Minos, not be very angry with you when he learns that you helped me to kill the Minotaur and escape from the palace?"

32

Ariadne agreed that her father would indeed be very angry when he realised that she had helped Theseus and the young Athenians. If all went according to plan, and Theseus managed to kill the Minotaur, she too would have to escape on the ship with while sails. She would have to sail with Theseus to Athens.

The next day, the dungeon guards came to feed one of the Athenians to the Minotaur. They opened the thick wooden door in the dungeon wall, and a horrible smell rolled out. Theseus volunteered to be the first to enter the Labyrinth. The guards were so astonished – no one had ever volunteered before – that they failed to notice the gleaming sword and a large ball of wool hidden beneath his now-bulging cloak.

Theseus walked through the doorway into the Labyrinth and the thick wooden door shut behind him with a dull thud. Carefully, with shaking hands, he tied the end of the large ball of wool to a nail in the doorpost. He them started to feel his way slowly and cautiously along the twisting and branching tunnels, turning first to the left and then to the right and always unrolling the wool as he walked. He was searching for the Minotaur. He wanted to find the creature before it found him.

The Labyrinth was a horrible place; very dark, very hot and very smelly. The tunnels seemed endless, and his footsteps crunched unpleasantly as he walked. Theseus suspected that he was walking on the bones of the Minotaur's victims. Soon Theseus lost all sense of time and direction. He felt that he had been walking for many hours. He could see nothing, but he could hear a far-away noise which, as he moved through the tunnels, grew louder and louder. It was the sound of a roaring bull.

At last, as he felt his way round yet another corner, Theseus saw a distant glimmer of light. He must be nearing the heart of the Labyrinth, the home of the Minotaur. Steadily, Theseus made his way towards the light, always remembering to create a trail by unrolling his wool. As he walked and walked, the ball of wool in his hand grew smaller and smaller, the light grew brighter and brighter, and the roaring noise grew louder and louder.

Turning one last corner, Theseus reached the heart of the Labyrinth. He saw stone pillars, lit torches, human bones, and something large and fierce charging straight at him. Theseus had found the Minotaur, and the Minotaur had seen Theseus. Dropping the now tiny ball of wool Theseus grasped his gleaming sword in both hands, and plunged it straight into the Minotaur's neck. With one final, very loud roar, the Minotaur died. Trembling, Theseus stepped over the Minotaur's body, and picked up his little ball of wool. He was easily able to followed the wool trail back through the twisting and branching tunnels, toward the dungeon door.

Opening the door, Theseus found Princess Ariadne waiting for him,

with the seven young women and six young men whom he had saved from being eaten by the Minotaur. The young Athenians let out a cheer when they saw Theseus, but there was no time to celebrate. They needed to escape from Crete before King Minos realised that his Minotaur had been killed. Quickly the young people ran to the harbour and boarded their ship. Soon they were sailing across the Mediterranean Sea, safe on their way back to Athens.

Theseus was so excited by his victory over the Minotaur, that he forgot his promise to change the ship's ships sails from black to white. And so, when King Aegeus looked across the sea and saw the Athenian ship returning with black sails, he assumed that his beloved son had been killed by the Minotaur. Filled with sadness, he threw himself off the cliff into the sea, and died. The place where King Aegeus died is today known as the Aegean Sea.

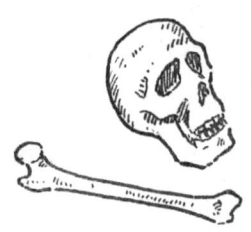

ABOUT THESEUS'S STORY

The Minotaur lives on Crete; a large island in the Mediterranean Sea. More than 600,000 people live on the island of Crete today, and many others visit each year to spend a holiday there.

Almost four thousand years ago there was a large palace at Knossos, on the island of Crete. Today this ancient palace is a ruin, but once it included many rooms, including workshops and storerooms. The people who lived in the Knossos palace worshipped bulls, and they decorated the palace walls with paintings of athletes jumping over bulls. That must have been a very dangerous sport! However, there is no Labyrinth under the Knossos palace, and the legend of King Minos and his Minotaur is not a true story.

WHAT DO YOU THINK?

1. Can you find the island of Crete on a map? And Athens?

2. What did the Minotaur look like? You may like to draw him.

3. Why did Ariadne give Theseus a large ball of wool?

4. Why did King Aegeus die?

4

ICARUS FLIES NEAR THE SUN

Daedalus was a good and clever man. He was an inventor and an architect who had designed and built many beautiful buildings during his long life. Unfortunately, Daedalus lived on the island of Crete, where he was forced to work for cruel King Minos. Do you remember the story of Prince Theseus who killed the Minotaur? Daedalus was the architect of the Labyrinth; the huge maze of twisting and branching tunnels where the Minotaur lived and ate his victims.

Daedalus had been ordered to build the Labyrinth, but he had no idea what it was to be used for. When he realised what was happening under the royal palace, he was horrified. He wanted to kill the Minotaur, but did not know how to do this. So he had a secret conversation with the good Princess Ariadne. He explained that the only way anyone could escape from the Labyrinth would be to use a ball of wool to create a trail back to the door. Ariadne remembered this good advice. She gave Theseus both a gleaming sword and a large ball of wool, and so helped him to defeat the Minotaur.

When King Minos realised that his Minotaur was dead he flew into a tremendous rage. He wanted to punish everyone who had helped Theseus. He could not punish his daughter, Princess Ariadne, because she had escaped on the ship with black sails. But he could punish his architect, Daedalus, who must surely have helped Ariadne and Theseus to kill the Minotaur. Minos locked Daedalus and his young son Icarus in a high tower in the royal palace. Here, Daedalus started to plot their escape from cruel King Minos and the island of Crete.

Daedalus knew that to be truly safe, he and Icarus must cross the Mediterranean Sea. But they could not swim away from Crete, because the distance was too far. And they could not escape by boat, because Minos commanded a big fleet of fast ships. He would easily be able to sail after them and kill them both. There was only one way to escape from the palace on the island of Crete. They must fly across the sky. And so, Daedalus designed and made two enormous pairs of wings. The wings were made from wax, and covered in feathers, which Daedalus collected from the birds that flew around the high tower window.

After many days of hard work, the wings were ready. It was time to escape from Crete. Daedalus tied the first pair of wings firmly onto Icarus's arms, and the second pair onto his own. He then turned to Icarus, and spoke to him sternly:

"Listen to me carefully Icarus, my son. These wings will allow us to jump out of the window. If we flap our arms up and down we will be able to fly like birds. We will travel across the sea, away from wicked King Minos and the island of Crete. We can start a new life somewhere else, and Minos will not be able to find us. But there is one very important thing that you must remember as we make our escape. These wings are made

from wax. They are strong, but they will melt in the heat of the sun. It is very important that you do not fly too high in the sky. If you do, the heat of the sun will melt your wings, and you will fall into the sea. I will not be able to save you. You must follow me, and always remember to fly low."

Icarus agreed, but he was not really listening to his Dad. He was humming a little tune, and thinking how splendid it would be to fly high in the sky like a bird or a god. He could not wait to try out his new wings. Daedalus was very worried; he knew that Icarus never listened to good advice, but this was their only possible means of escape. Again and again, he repeated that Icarus must not fly too high, towards the sun.

Now the moment had come to escape. First Daedalus, then Icarus, jumped out of the tower window and flapped their arms quickly up and down. And away they flew like birds. Leaving the high tower far behind they zoomed across the island of Crete then across the blue Mediterranean Sea, towards safety.

Daedalus flew low, and at first Icarus followed his father obediently. But after an hour or so of safe but dull flying, Icarus was very bored. He wanted to enjoy himself. He wanted to swoop, and to dive, and to loop-the-loop. He wanted to fly high into the sky like a bird or a god. Again and again, Daedalus warned his son to be careful and to fly low, but Icarus would not listen. With a shout of pleasure, he flew higher and higher into the sky, aiming straight at the sun.

And, of course, his wax wings started to melt in the heat. As the wax dripped into the sea, and the feathers fluttered down like snow, Icarus found that he could no longer fly. He flapped and flapped his arms, but this no longer worked. With a terrible scream, he tumbled from the sky. Icarus fell into the sea and vanished beneath the waves. Crying, Daedalus flew low, searching for his beloved son, but Icarus had gone. There was nothing that Daedalus could do to save him.

After many hours of searching Daedalus flew on alone. Eventually he reached the island of Sicily, where he was welcomed by the people. Daedalus lived for many years on Sicily, where he was respected as a wise man. But he never forgot his lost son, Icarus.

ABOUT ICARUS'S STORY

Daedalus made his wings from feathers, which he stuck into place with wax. He collected his feathers from the birds that flew around his high tower. He must have collected his wax from the bees that buzzed around the royal palace. Bees are very busy and useful insects. They fly around our fields and gardens feeding on the pollen and nectar provided by our flowers. This helps the flowers to grow. Back home at the beehive the bees make wax, which they use to build honeycombs; the nurseries where the young bees are raised. Bees also make honey, which they store in their honeycombs as food for the young bees. People like to eat honey, because it has a pleasant, sweet taste.

Ancient Greek and Roman schoolchildren did not write on paper, as we do today. They wrote on "writing tablets", which were made from pieces of wood covered in a layer of smooth wax. They scratched their words into the wax using a pointed stick known as a stylus. If they wanted to rub out their words, they simply melted the wax slightly. This smoothed out the wax and made the old words disappear. When the tablet had cooled, they were able to write new words on the wax surface. Today we use wax for the candles that we use to light our homes and decorate our birthday cakes.

You could try writing the Greek way, using modelling clay instead of wax. Smooth out the clay, then scratch your words using a pencil as your stylus. When you have finished your writing, you can smooth your your clay to rub out your words, and start all over again.

WHAT DO YOU THINK?

1. Daedalus is an inventor and an architect. Do you know what an architect is?

2. Which animal makes wax and honey?

3. Why does Icarus fall into the sea?

4. Can you draw a picture of Icarus and Daedalus flying in the sky?

5

ATALANTA RUNS A RACE

Atalanta was a very unusual princess. She did not like to sit in the cool palace sewing and gossiping with her friends, as other princesses did. Nor did she like to wear fashionable dresses or sparkling jewellery. She did not like to paint her eyes with colourful makeup, and she never asked her maids to arrange her hair in elaborate styles. In fact, she never wore makeup, she didn't like anyone to fuss with her hair, and she was not very keen on taking a bath, either.

Atalanta spent all her days outdoors, in the hot sunlight. She wore simple clothes in dull colours that allowed her to hide in the forest, and she tied her long hair back so it did not get in her eyes. Day after day Atalanta tracked the forest animals. By watching the animals, she learned how to fight like a bear, how to run fast like a deer, and how to swim like the fish in the forest streams. Atalanta loved to fight and run and swim, but best of all, she liked to hunt. She could weave a net to catch an animal, could throw a spear straight and true, and she was an expert shot with her bow and arrows. She was brave and fierce, and

she worshipped Artemis, the goddess of hunting.

One fine summer, the farmers gathered an unusually large harvest. The barns were stuffed to the rafters with grain and vegetable and fruit, and the vats were filled to the brim with oil and wine. The shepherds had raised many fine sheep in the fields, and the hunters and fishers had caught many wild animals, birds and fish. It was obvious that this year, no one would go hungry during the harsh winter months. The people decided to thank the gods and goddesses for their generosity. They thanked Demeter, the goddess of farming, they thanked Athena, the goddess of wisdom, and they thanked Dionysus, the god of the wine harvest. But they forgot to thank Artemis, the goddess of hunting. That was a bad mistake.

Artemis was very angry that the people had forgotten to thank her. She had worked hard for the people, and she deserved to be remembered. As a punishment, she sent a huge boar to terrorise the people. The huge boar rampaged through the land. It ate all the food stored in the barns, and drank all the oil and wine stored in the vats. It trampled the fields, uprooted the trees in the forest and killed many of the farmers. No one could stop the huge boar. It caused destruction wherever it went. Horrified, the people prayed to Artemis to beg her forgiveness, but she would not control her boar. Instead, she told the people that if they wanted to stop the boar, they must hunt and kill it.

A group of brave young hunters volunteered to catch the huge boar. They were all young men, with one exception. Atalanta joined the group. Some of the men were not happy about this. They believed that a girl could not hunt as well as a man. But Atalanta simply smiled to herself. She knew that she was exceptionally skilled with the bow and arrow, and she believed that she could help the young men to kill the huge boar.

The group set to work tracking the boar. Soon they had it cornered in a steep-sided valley, and they threw nets over the beast to stop it running away. The boar snorted with rage, but could not escape. It was trapped. One by one the young men stepped forward to shoot their arrows at the boar. Each young man hoped that he would be the hero who would kill the beast that had been terrorising the people and destroying their food. But the huge boar was protected by the goddess Artemis, and their arrows simply bounced off its thick hide. Finally, Atalanta stepped forward. She selected an arrow from the quiver on her back, and put it to her bow-string. Then she fired. Atalanta's arrow pierced the boar's thick hide, causing the beast to squeal in shock as it fell to the ground. The young men rushed forward waving their swords and spears, and soon the boar was no more. As a prize for being the first hunter to wound the huge boar, Atalanta was given the boar's skin and head.

Atalanta was now very famous. Princes from many lands wanted to marry her, but Atalanta did not want to marry anyone. She wanted to

continue being a hunter, and to spend her days in the forest with the wild animals. Her father, King Iasos, had other ideas. He wanted his daughter to marry a fine prince. He thought that this would make her happy. Atalanta did not want to disappoint her father, and so they reached an agreement. She would marry the first man to beat her in a running race. The race would be three laps of the race-track, and all the men who lost the race would be killed. King Iasos agreed, and hopeful young men started to arrive at the palace, eager to race against the famous hunting princess. Atalanta won all the races without even getting out of breath – she was very fast indeed – and all the young men were killed.

Hippomenes was a young man who was in love with Atalanta. He very much wanted to marry her, but he had seen just how fast she could run and, although he was an athlete, he knew that he was nowhere near fast enough to beat her in a race. He did not want to die racing against the hunting princess. And so he asked Aphrodite, the goddess of love, for help:

"Oh mighty Aphrodite; I am in love with the brave Atalanta. Please tell me how I may win the race at the race-track, and so claim her as my bride."

Aphrodite, who was very sympathetic to young lovers, decided to help Hippomenes. She gave him three beautiful golden apples:

"Here, Hippomenes. Take these three beautiful golden apples. No woman can resist them. These golden apples will help you to win the race, and so you will be able to claim your bride."

One the day of the race, Atalanta lined up next to Hippomenes. She liked to look of him, and for the first time she felt sorry that she was to beat him, and he was to die. King Iasos shouted "Go!", and they set off, running as fast as they could around the racetrack.

On the first lap of the track, Hippomenes ran level with Atalanta, and dropped one of the golden apples. Atalanta saw it roll away and, fascinated, stopped running to pick it up. She then ran even faster, and caught up with Hippomenes.

On the second lap of the track, the same thing happened. Hippomenes ran level with Atalanta and dropped a golden apple, and Atalanta stopped running to pick it up. She then ran even faster and caught up with Hippomenes again.

On the third lap of the track – you have guessed it – Hippomenes ran level with Atalanta and dropped the third golden apple. But this apple was larger and heavier than the others, and he threw it away from him so that it rolled a long way away from the race-track. Atalanta hesitated; she knew that she should concentrate on winning the race, but she really wanted that third golden apple. She could not resist the temptation. She ran off the track to collect the golden apple. Although she then ran faster than she had ever run before, she had left it too late. She could not catch up. Panting and puffing, Hippomenes won the race and Atalanta came second.

Hippomenes and Atalanta were married, and had a very happy life together.

ABOUT ATALANTA'S STORY

The ancient Greeks were very fond of sporting competitions and races. About 3000 years ago they started the Olympic Games in a city called Olympia. These games were held every four years to honour the king of the gods, Zeus. The earliest games included just one event: a running race around a running-track, Gradually, as the years went by, more and more sports were added to the Olympic Games. These new sports included jumping, throwing, boxing, wrestling and chariot racing. Women and girls were not allowed to compete in the ancient games, and married women were not even allowed to watch them. The last ancient Olympic Games was held in 393 CE.

For many years, there were no Olympic Games. Then, in 1896 they started again in Athens, the capital city of Greece. Today, the Olympic Games are held every four years, in cities throughout the world. Many hundreds of men and women from over 200 nations compete in many hundreds of competitions and races, and everyone is allowed to watch. The official symbol of the games is five coloured rings representing Africa, Asia, Australia, Europe and the Americas.

WHAT DO YOU THINK?

1. What kind of animal is a boar?

2. Who is the Greek goddess of hunting?

3. What prize did Atalanta receive for being the first hunter to wound the huge boar?

4. How many golden apples did Hippomenes drop in the race?

6

MIDAS IS UNLUCKY

King Midas was a kind but very foolish man. He lived in a splendid palace with his beautiful wife and their lovely young daughter Zoë. He spent his days dressed in fine clothes, eating tasty foods, and drinking delicious wines and fruit juices. But Midas was not as happy as he should have been, because he thought that he had a problem. His imaginary problem was a very silly one. Midas was rich. He was far richer than all his friends and neighbours, but he worried that he was not rich enough. Midas wanted to be the richest man in the world. He longed for a never-ending supply of gold.

One day, Midas found a stranger wandering lost in the woods near his palace. The stranger was old and confused, and he did not know where he was. He did not even know who he was. Midas kindly invited the confused old man to stay in his palace. He dressed the old man in clean clothes, and gave him plenty to eat and drink and a comfortable bed to sleep in. Ten days later, much to Midas' surprise, Dionysus, the god of the wine harvest, arrived at the palace to collect the old man. Dionysus explained to Midas that the stranger was his old teacher, Silenus. The god thanked the king for caring for Silenus and, as a reward, allowed Midas to make one wish. Immediately, and without thinking, Midas blurted out "Oh – I wish that everything I touch would turn to gold."

Dionysus felt that this was not a very sensible wish, but he did as Midas asked. He granted the wish, and took Silenus away.

Having waved the god and the old man goodbye, Midas decided to try out his new superpower. He walked into the palace garden, stretched out his arm, and touched the green leaf on a tree. Immediately, the whole tree became a golden tree statue. Overjoyed, Midas wandered through his garden, randomly touching the trees, the flowers and even the stones in the path. Soon, almost everything in the garden was made of gleaming gold.

Growing hungry, Midas ordered the servants to prepare a magnificent feast of roast lamb, vegetables and olives, to be washed down with fine wines and fruit juices. But, as he sat at the table, his wooden chair immediately turned to gold. Midas started to realise that he had a problem. He could not eat the tasty food because it became gold in his hands, and no one can eat gold. And he could not drink the delicious wines and fruit juices because they turned to liquid gold when they touched his lips, and no one can drink liquid gold. Worried, and now very hungry and very thirsty, he was wondering if he was

going to starve to death, when his young daughter Zoë ran up to him. Midas shouted at her to stop, but she did not hear him. She flung her arms around her father's neck to hug him. Immediately, Zoë was transformed from a living girl into a beautiful golden statue.

King Midas was so upset, he started to cry. He now realised that, although he had all the gold that anyone could ever want, it was not making him happy. He had been far happier before Dionysus granted his wish. In fact, he now hated the sight of gold. And so he prayed to the god to have the gift of gold removed.

Dionysus heard Midas's prayer, and felt very sorry for him. He knew that Midas was not a bad man, merely a foolish one, and he remembered that Midas had been very kind to old Silenus. He decided to help the king get rid of his golden touch. Dionysus told Midas to leave the palace and walk to the river. Here he was to wash his hands in the cold water. Midas followed his instructions, and walked to the river leaving a trail of golden footprints behind him. As he plunged his hands into the cold river water he felt the golden power flow out of his body, turning the brown river sands to gold. Midas stopped washing his hands and, hopefully, tried touching a leaf on a tree. This time, to his huge relief, the leaf remained green and the tree remained wooden.

Hurrying back to the palace, Midas saw that the trail of golden footprints had vanished, and that the palace garden was no longer

gleaming. The trees were living trees once again, the flowers were real flowers, and the stones in the path were real stones. Best of all, his young daughter Zoë ran towards him, alive once again. She flung her arms around her father's neck, and they had a big hug. Then the entire family then sat down to enjoy a magnificent feast of roast lamb,

vegetables and olives, washed down with fine wines and fruit juices.

King Midas had learned a harsh lesson. He now hated the sight of gold, and he no longer had any wish to be wealthy. Instead, he developed the ambition to become a great musician. He started to study music with the god Pan, who was an expert in playing the reed pipes.

The god Pan thought that he was the best musician amongst the gods. But the god Apollo, an expert in playing the lyre, thought that he was the best musician amongst the gods. Pan and Apollo decided to hold a competition to decide who was the best musician. They would each play a tune, and a judge would award a prize for the best performance. Pan and Apollo chose King Midas as the competition judge.

A large audience assembled, Midas sat at the judge's desk, and the competition began. First Pan played a lovely tune on his reed pipes, then Apollo played a lovely tune on his lyre. The audience clapped and cheered for Pan, but they clapped and cheered much louder for Apollo. Apollo was the audience's favourite musician; he should have won the prize. But Midas foolishly decided to award the prize for the best performance to his friend and teacher, Pan.

Apollo was very angry. He had really wanted to win the music competition. He knew that he was the better musician, and he knew that the king had deliberately given the prize to his own friend, Pan. Apollo cursed Midas, shouting that he could not have listened to the music properly, because he had the ears of a donkey. And instantly, Midas grew a pair of long, hairy donkey ears. Apollo laughed and laughed, the audience laughed and laughed, and even Pan smiled a bit. King Midas looked very silly with his new ears.

Midas did not laugh. He was horrified and embarrassed by his long, hairy donkey ears. He tried to hide them by always wearing a very tall hat. This worked quite well but, of course, he had to take his hat off when he had his hair cut. Apart from the queen, the royal barber was therefore the only person in the land who knew that King Midas had donkey ears. The barber was told that he must not, under any circumstances, tell anyone about the king's unusual ears. But the barber was a very talkative man, and he found it difficult to keep such an interesting secret. So, driven mad by his desire to tell someone – anyone – that King Midas had donkey ears, the barber thought of a plan.

Late one night, the royal barber crept out of the palace. He ran to the river bank and, having looked around nervously to make sure that no one was watching, dug a deep hole in the ground. He then bent over, stuck his head right into the hole, and whispered the secret that he had been longing to tell: "King Midas has donkey's ears". Immediately, the barber felt much better. He returned to the palace, and never spoke about the king's ears again. But, a few weeks later a thick bed of reeds grew in the hole near the river. And all day, every day, as the wind blew,

the reeds whispered: "King Midas has donkey's ears". Soon, everyone in the land knew Midas' embarrassing secret.

ABOUT MIDAS'S STORY

The ancient Greeks enjoyed music, singing and dancing just as much as we do today. Their musicians played at weddings, funerals, religious ceremonies and banquets, and musicians even competed at the Olympic Games. Music was taught in schools, and good musicians were highly respected.

King Midas is asked to judge an important music competition. His friend and teacher, Pan, plays the reed pipes or syrinx; a wind instrument made from four or more reeds or pipes of different length, tied in a row. Pan would have played his tune by holding his instrument in both hands, and blowing across the top of the pipes. It is possible to make a similar noise by blowing across the top of a bottle: ask a grown-up to show you how this is done.

The god Apollo plays the lyre. This is a stringed instrument that looks something like a modern harp or zither. It has seven or more strings, which are plucked by the musician. Often the lyre player sings as he or she plays the tune. Other popular Greek instruments included the rattle, cymbals and drums.

WHAT DO YOU THINK?

1. Who is Dionysus?

2. What is King Midas' daughter called?

3. King Midas wished that everything he touched would turn to gold. Why was that a silly wish?

4. What job does a barber do?

7

PERSEUS KILLS A GORGON

Acrisius was the king of Argos. He had just one child; a grown-up daughter named Danaë. Danaë too had just one child; a young son named Perseus. Perseus's father was Zeus, the king of the gods.

One day, as Acrisius prayed to the gods in the temple, he received a message. It was not the sort of message that anyone would want to hear. The gods told Acrisius that he would one day be killed by his own grandson. Frightened for his own safety, but unwilling to harm either his daughter Danaë or her young son Perseus, Acrisius ordered his carpenters to make a large wooden chest. He forced Danaë and Perseus to lie in the chest, then he slammed the lid shut, locked it, and threw the chest into the Mediterranean Sea. As the chest floated away from Argos, Acrisius felt a great sense of relief. With Perseus gone, he had no grandson. And with Danaë gone, he could never have another grandson. Problem solved! There was now no way that he could be killed. He would live for ever.

Locked in the dark chest, bobbing up and down with the waves, Danaë and Perseus were very frightened. They thought that they were about to drown. Or, if they did not drown, that they would starve to death in the chest. They did not realise that Zeus, king of the gods and father of Perseus, was protecting them from danger. After several days at sea, their locked chest washed up on the shore of the island of Seriphos, and Danaë and Perseus were rescued by a kind fisherman. They went to live in the fisherman's cottage, where Perseus grew up to become a good and brave fisherman.

The island of Seriphos was ruled by King Polydectes. Polydectes fell in love with Danaë; he wanted to marry her and to make her his queen. Perseus, however, did not trust Polydectes. He realised that the king was a cruel man, and he did not want him to marry his mother and become his father. Perseus asked Danaë not to marry Polydectes, and she agreed. She would do as her son asked. This interference in his love life made Polydectes very angry indeed. If Perseus vanished, Danaë would probably agree to be his bride. Polydectes started to think of ways that Perseus could be forced to leave the island of Seriphos.

King Polydectes announced that he was going to throw a splendid party. There would be vast amounts of excellent food, many kinds of delicious drinks, and some very good entertainment provided by the best musicians, singers, dancers and acrobats on Seriphos. All the young men on the island were to be invited to the party. However, every guest would be expected to bring a horse as a gift for the king.

Perseus was very excited because he, too, was invited to the king's party. He could not wait to eat the excellent food, drink the delicious drinks, and enjoy the musicians, singers, dancers and acrobats. There was only one problem; he was a humble fisherman, and he did not have a horse to give to the king. Foolishly, he went to Polydectes, and explained his problem:

"I am so sorry, my king. I really want to come to your splendid party, but I do not have a horse to give to you. However, I will give you anything else that you ask for. Anything at all. Just tell me what you would like."

Polydectes thought for a moment, and then spoke. His response horrified Perseus:

"Perseus, you have offered to bring me anything that I ask for. So, I ask you to bring me the head of Medusa, the snake-haired Gorgon whose eyes turn living creatures to stone. Go now, and collect the head. Do not return to the island of Seriphos until you have this gift for me."

Perseus went pale. He felt a bit sick, and he started to tremble. He knew exactly who Medusa was. She was one of the three Gorgon sisters who lived in a faraway land. The three sisters were named Euryale, Stheno and Medusa. All three had human faces and arms. But they also had metal claws, hair made from live snakes, and the lower body of a giant serpent. All three were very dangerous, and all three liked to kill. Just one glance from their eyes would turn any living creature into a stone statue. Only one of the three Gorgon sisters – Medusa – was mortal and could be killed. The other two Gorgon sisters, Euryale and Stheno, could not die.

Extremely worried, Perseus prayed to the wise goddess Athena and asked for her help. Luckily, Athena liked Perseus, and was happy to offer some good advice. First, she told Perseus that he would need to collect the right equipment if he was to kill the Gorgon. She lent him a polished metal shield. His father Zeus, king of the gods, lent him sharp sword, and Hermes, the messenger god, lent a pair of winged sandals which would allow Perseus to fly, and a helmet that would allow him to become invisible.

Next, the wise goddess Athena told Perseus how to find Medusa:

"You must first travel to the house of the Grey Ones. They will tell you where to find the home of the Gorgons."

"But who are the Grey Ones?" asked Perseus, "and where do they live?"

"The Grey Ones are three very old women. They are the sisters of the Gorgons, but they are harmless. They live in a house many miles from here. They share one eye and one tooth, passing them from one to another as they need to use them. You must sneak into their house, steal their one eye, and refuse to give it back until they tell you where Medusa lives."

Perseus strapped on his sandals, put on his invisibility helmet, picked up his sharp sword and polished shield, and flew off to find the far-away house where the Grey Ones lived. Eventually, after many days and nights of searching, he found it. The house was damp and dark, and it smelt quite unpleasant. Entering without knocking, Perseus saw the three very old women crouched around a small fire. These were the Grey Ones. The first very old woman held an eye in her withered hand; she could see, but she could not eat. The second very old woman held a tooth in her withered hand; she could eat, but she could not see. The third very old woman held nothing at all in her withered hand; she had no eye and no tooth, and could neither see nor eat.

Perseus rushed forward, and snatched the eye from the first Grey One. Immediately, all three sisters shrieked loudly:

"Who is that? Who has stolen our one eye? Give it back at once, you thief! Without that eye, none of us can see."

"I am Perseus, son of Danaë. I come from the island of Seriphos. I mean you no harm. I will gladly return your eye. But first you must tell me where the Gorgon known as Medusa lives."

Grumbling, the three very old women told Perseus where he might find Medusa's home. Perseus returned the stolen eye to the nearest old woman, and quickly flew away from the house of the Grey Ones.

Medusa and her two Gorgon sisters lived in a cave cut into the slope of a very steep mountain, near the sea. The cave looked like a simple hole in the rock, but Perseus knew that he had found the right place, because the cave entrance was surrounded by many, many statues. These were the men, women, children and animals who had accidentally looked at the Gorgons, and had instantly been turned into stone.

Perseus tiptoed past the many statues, and entered the cave. Inside, he could see columns, stairways, and many rooms, and he could hear a curious rumbling and hissing noise. The three Gorgons were asleep. All three sisters were snoring very loudly, while the live snakes that covered their heads were hissing quietly as they dreamed. Perseus followed the sound of the snoring and hissing because he knew that it would lead him to Medusa and her sisters. However, he also knew that he must not look directly at the three Gorgons, as their eyes had the power to turn him into stone. He did not want to become a part of their statue collection. So, he used his polished shield as a mirror, and looked only at the reflections in the cave as he made his way cautiously towards their bedroom, being careful not to trip on the stone statues that littered the floor.

Medusa was the largest and ugliest of the three sisters. Not only did she have a slithery serpent body, metal claws and live-snake hair, she also had a large tongue that flickered in and out of her mouth, and a very mean expression on her face. Creeping towards the sleeping

Medusa, and always using his shield as a mirror, Perseus drew his sword. He was just about to strike a fatal blow, when the live snakes on Medusa's head let out a loud hiss, and Medusa woke up. She opened one eye, then the other eye, and looked around her, but Perseus, who was still wearing his invisibility helmet and still using the shield as a mirror, was safe. Confused, Medusa reared up, and Perseus swung his sharp sword. The hair-snakes continued to hiss, but Medusa was dead. Perseus picked up her head by its snake-hair, and dropped it into a bag. He then flew away, quickly, before the other two Gorgons could wake up and turn him to stone.

Safely back on the island of Seriphos, Perseus returned his equipment to Athena, Zeus and Hermes and thanked them for their help. He then went to straight the palace, and demanded an audience with the king.

"Ah, Perseus," Polydectes laughed. "Welcome back to the island of Seriphos. What is in your bag? Is it a gift for me? Have you bought me the head of Medusa, as you promised?"

"Indeed I have, my king" said Perseus. And, closing his eyes tight shut, he quickly pulled Medusa's head out of the bag, again holding it by the snake-hair. Astonished, Polydectes looked directly into Medusa's eyes, and was instantly turned to stone. Carefully, with his eyes still tight shut, Perseus put the head back into the bag.

With Polydectes now a statue, Danaë was free to marry the kind fisherman who had rescued her and her son many years ago. But what happened to King Acrisius of Argos? Did he live forever, as he had hoped? No. No one can live for ever. One day Acrisius was watching a sporting competition when a discus flew into the crowd, hit him on the head, and killed him. The discus that accidentally killed King Acrisius was thrown by his long-lost grandson, Perseus.

ABOUT PERSEUS'S STORY

Perseus uses a sharp sword to cut off Medusa's head. He also carries a polished metal shield. Normally a shield would be used to protect a soldier in battle, but Perseus uses his shield as a mirror. Because he never looks directly at Medusa, but always looks at her reflection in the polished shield, he is not turned into a stone statue.

Perseus borrows his sword and shield from the god Zeus and the goddess Athena. Most ancient Greek soldiers had to pay for their own weapons and armour. However, a soldier whose father had died in battle was allowed to use his own father's equipment. The Greek foot soldiers, who were known as "hoplites", carried a tall spear, a short sword, and a large round shield made of wood and metal, which was known as a "hoplon". They wore a helmet, a breast plate and greaves (a kind of shin pad) for protection. In battle the hoplites stood in a line with their shields overlapping, and marched forwards together as a team. The enemy would see what looked like a moving wall of shields, armed with dangerous spears.

In addition to the hoplites, the ancient Greek army also included archers who fought with a bow and arrows, and a cavalry, who rode horses. All the Greek soldiers were men; women were not allowed to fight.

WHAT DO YOU THINK?

1. Who is Hermes?

2. What pieces of equipment do the gods and goddesses lend to Perseus?

3. How many eyes and teeth do the three Grey Ones have?

4. Medusa has the body of a great slithery serpent, the head of a woman, and hissing snake-hair. Can you draw her?

8

ARACHNE WEAVES A WEB

Arachne was the daughter of a shepherd who lived in the land of Lydia. She was a very clever girl. She could read, write, and do very difficult sums. She could care for the sheep in the fields, could clean the house, and could cook a tasty meal for her family. But the thing that she did best of all, was to weave colourful wool into beautiful tapestries. Every day Arachne sat at her loom in the shepherd's hut, and created works of art in wool. People came from far and wide to look at Arachne's beautiful tapestries, and to watch her as she worked. This made Arachne feel very proud and important.

Unfortunately, Arachne was not a nice girl. She was vain and big-headed, and every day as she sat at her loom, she boasted about her skill at weaving. She thought that she was almost certainly the best weaver in Lydia. In fact, she was probably the best weaver in the world. The people who came day after day to watch Arachne work at her loom agreed with her. She was indeed the best weaver in the world: there was no one better. Surely the great goddess Athena herself must have taught

Arachne how to weave such beautiful tapestries.

Most girls would be flattered by the suggestion that they had been taught by the great goddess Athena. Arachne, however, was not at all flattered:

"Taught by Athena? No way! I make far better tapestries than Athena. She should be taking lessons from me. I could teach her a thing or two."

The great goddess Athena heard Arachne's boast, and was not amused. She decided to visit the girl, and offer her some good advice. Disguising herself as a poor old woman bent over a walking stick, Athena travelled to the shepherd's hut in Lydia, where Arachne lived with her family. The poor old woman stood beside Arachne, and watched her as she worked. Arachne was using brightly coloured wool to create a beautiful picture on her loom. And, as usual, she was boasting. First she boasted that she was the best weaver in Lydia. Then she boasted that she was the best weaver in the whole world. Finally, she went much too far, and boasted that she was a better weaver than the great goddess Athena herself.

The poor old woman spoke. "Be careful what you say, Arachne. You are indeed a skilful weaver, but you are not as skilled as the great goddess Athena. Do not insult the goddess by comparing yourself to her. If she hears what you are saying, she will punish you. Apologise to her at once, and all will be well."

Arachne looked up from her loom, and saw the old poor woman standing before her, bent over her walking stick. She did not think that the old woman was anyone important, and so she did not feel the need to be polite to her:

"Shut up, you stupid old woman. Who cares what you think? Why should I apologise for my words? I know that I am the best weaver in the world. Of course I am better than the great goddess Athena. If the great goddess was here, now, I would challenge her to a weaving competition. And I would easily win. But the great goddess Athena is too frightened to compete with me; she is a coward."

Hearing these words, the poor old woman dropped hers stick, stood upright and transformed herself back into the great goddess Athena. Arachne was so shocked that she jumped to her feet – she had not expected that to happen – but she did not apologise for her rudeness and beg for forgiveness. Indeed, her words became even more rude.

"Greetings Athena. I am so glad that you have come to my home. We must have a weaving competition to prove to everyone that I am a much better weaver than you. Maybe I could give you some weaving lessons!"

Athena was very angry. She was not used to such disrespect from a young girl. So she raised her arm, pointed her finger, and a new loom appeared beside Arachne's own. The goddess and the girl sat down at their looms, and each started to weave the colourful wool into beautiful

74

pictures. They worked fast, their fingers flying over the looms.

The great goddess Athena wove a picture that showed the gods and goddesses punishing foolish men and women. At the centre of her picture stood Athena herself, dressed in glittering armour. Arachne also

wove a picture of the gods and goddesses. But in her picture the gods were doing foolish and stupid things: she hoped that her picture would embarrass Athena and make her feel foolish.

The tapestries were completed, and the competition ended. And there was no doubt about it. Arachne's tapestry was very good indeed, but Athena's tapestry was much, much better. It was perfect. Athena was, without doubt, the better weaver. Arachne realised that she had lost the competition, and she started to worry. She had been very foolish, had said some very silly things, and had offended the great goddess. What would happen to her?

Athena looked at Arachne's tapestry, and smiled. The she raised her arm, and pointed her finger at Arachne. At once, the girl started to shrink. Her hair and teeth fell out, her eyes started to bulge and she grew four extra limbs. She had been transformed into a large spider! Terrified, Arachne scuttled across the floor of the hut, and tried to hide in a dark and dusty corner. Here she started to weave: not a beautiful, colourful tapestry, but a large spider's web.

ABOUT ARACHNE'S STORY

The girls and women of ancient Greece had to learn how to spin wool into thread, and then how to weave that thread into cloth. They were responsible for providing their families with clothing, bed sheets, rugs and tapestries.

The wool was gathered from the sheep. It was made into one long thread by twisting it together. This twisting process was known as spinning. The spun thread was often wound into a ball. You may remember that Ariadne gave Theseus a ball of wool to help him escape from the Labyrinth.

This spun thread was woven on a loom to make cloth. The loom was a wooden frame attached to a wall. Many threads were tied to the top of the frame, and allowed to hang down. These were called the warp threads. The weaver then threaded strands of wool through the warp threads, going over one thread, then under the next, then over the next, and so on. After many hours of very hard work, this made a piece of woollen cloth, or tapestry. A skilled weaver could use coloured wools to weave a picture into her tapestry.

You could try making a very simple loom by taking a pencil or a ruler, and tying woollen threads around it. These are your warp threads. Then, take a new thread and weave it over, and under, and over, and under the warp threads until a small piece of cloth develops.

WHAT DO YOU THINK?

1. Who is Athena?

2. Which animal provided Arachne with wool?

3. What equipment does Arachne use to weave her tapestry?

4. Arachne is transformed into a spider. Do you know how many legs
   a spider has?

9

OEDIPUS MEETS THE SPHINX

Many years ago, the kingdom of Thebes was ruled by King Laius and Queen Jocasta. Laius and Jocasta were very happy, and they grew even happier when Jocasta gave birth to a healthy baby boy. Laius went to the temple to thank the gods for his good fortune; his happy and healthy life, his lovely wife and their new baby son. But while he was praying in the temple, he received a shocking message from the gods. His future had been foretold. Laius would one day be killed by his own son.

Frightened, Laius rushed home, seized the baby boy, and rode off into the countryside with him. Laius abandoned his new son under a tree on a mountain in the far-away land of Corinth, He returned home believing that, with the baby gone, he would now be safe from harm.

Alone on the mountain, cold and hungry, the baby boy cried and cried. His wailing attracted the attention of a group of shepherds. The shepherds found the tiny baby boy lying under the tree, and picked him up. Puzzled, they took him to Polybus, king of Corinth. As no one came

forward to claim the baby, Polybus, who had no children of his own, decided to adopt the lad. He named the baby Oedipus, and raised him in the palace as his own son.

Oedipus had a very happy childhood, living in the Corinth palace with King Polybus. He grew up to become a fine and brave young man. One day, Oedipus went to the temple to thank the gods for his good fortune; his happy and healthy life and his kind father. But while he was praying in the temple, he received a shocking message from the gods. His future had been foretold. Oedipus would one day kill his own father.

Oedipus did not know that he had been adopted as a baby. He believed that King Polybus was his father, and he certainly did not want to kill him. He loved Polybus and wanted to protect him from harm. Oedipus therefore decided to leave Corinth immediately. He said a sad goodbye to Polybus, to Corinth and its people, and set off walking along the long, steep mountain path that led towards the kingdom of Thebes.

As he walked along the steep mountain path towards Thebes, Oedipus was almost flattened by an old man driving a chariot at a dangerously fast speed. This made him very angry. Oedipus ran after the chariot, and shouted insults at the driver. The driver shouted some rude words back, and the quarrel quickly turned into a fight that ended with the old man lying dead on the mountain path. Oedipus buried the body, and continued on his long walk to Thebes. Soon he had forgotten

all about the fight. But unknown to him, the dead old man was his real father, King Laius of Thebes. Even though they did not know it, Oedipus had killed his own father, and Laius had been killed by his own son.

Further along the path, just outside the kingdom of Thebes, Oedipus met the creature known as the Sphinx. She was a frightening sight. She had the head of a beautiful woman, the body of a lion, the wings of an eagle and the tail of a snake. She was sitting with her huge body

blocking the path, so that no one could squeeze past her. No one could enter or leave Thebes without passing the Sphinx.

The Sphinx was mean. She forced all the travellers who wished to enter or leave Thebes to listen to a riddle. Those who succeeded in solving the riddle were allowed to go on their way. Those who failed to solve the riddle were eaten. So far, no one had succeeded in solving the riddle; everyone had been eaten. Oedipus could not help noticing that the Sphinx was sitting on quite a large pile of human bones.

Now it was his turn to listen to the riddle, and attempt to solve it.

"What creature speaks with one voice, yet walks on four legs in the morning, two legs in the afternoon, and three legs at night?"

Oedipus thought long and hard. He scratched his head, rubbed his nose, and scratched his head again. Finally, he had an answer.

"People. They speak with one voice throughout their lives, yet they crawl on four limbs when they are babies, walk on two legs for most of their grown-up life, then use a walking stick as a third leg when they are old."

The Sphinx was both impressed and annoyed: she was hungry, and had wanted to eat the tasty-looking young man. Now she could not.

"Well done Oedipus. You are quite right. You may go on your way."

She stood up, and suddenly threw herself over the edge of the path, vanishing out of sight.

Finally, hot, thirsty and with aching feet, Oedipus entered the kingdom of Thebes. The people of Thebes were so impressed that Oedipus had been able to make the Sphinx go away, that they made him their new king.

ABOUT OEDIPUS'S STORY

The Sphinx asks Oedipus to solve a riddle; she is quite cross when he is successful, because she had wanted to eat him.

The ancient Greeks were very fond of riddles and jokes. Here is one of their jokes:

A man visits a talkative barber. When the barber asks how he wants his hair cutting, the man tells him "silently".

Here are some modern riddles and jokes for you to enjoy:

Q: Which school subject is best when you are hungry?
A: History, because it is full of dates

Q: Why didn't Oedipus like to eat his chips?
A: Because they were fried in ancient Greece

Q: Oedipus is an ancient Greek name. Can you spell it?
A: IT

WHAT DO YOU THINK?

1. Why did King Laius leave his new baby son under a tree on a mountain in the far-away land of Corinth?

2. Who killed King Laius?

3. The Sphinx is a frightening creature with the head of a woman, the body of a lion, the wings of an eagle and the tail of a snake. Can you draw her?

4. Do you have a favourite joke or riddle? Tell it to your friends or family, and see if you can make everyone laugh.

10

ROMULUS BUILDS A CITY

Many years ago, Numitor ruled the ancient Italian city of Alba Longa. Numitor was a good man and a good king, but not everyone was happy with his reign. His brother Amulius, a mean and jealous man, thought that he should be king of Alba Longa. Amulius gathered an army of supporters, and forced his brother Numitor off the throne. Amulius now ruled Alba Longa as king. Amulius lived in the royal place, while Numitor was forced to live in a damp cave, outside the city walls. The people of Alba Longa were not happy with this new arrangement, and they did not like their new king. But they could not do anything about it.

Numitor had a daughter named Rhea Silvia, and Rhea Silvia had twin baby sons named Romulus and Remus. Their father was Mars, the powerful god of war and farming. Amulius did not want the twin boys to grow up. He was worried that they might raise an army and fight for the throne of Alba Longa. He therefore ordered that Romulus and Remus should be killed, and that Rhea Silvia should be kept prisoner in a locked room.

A servant did as Amulius asked. He took Rhea Silvia, and locked her in a room. He then placed the twin boys in a basket, and carried them out of the city of Alba Longa. He abandoned the basket on the bank of the River Tiber, and hurried back to the palace to report that the babies would soon be dead.

However, the baby boys were not destined to die. They had been discovered by the kind river god Tiberinus, who had heard them crying on the bank of his river. Tiberinus felt sorry for the two helpless baby boys. He decided that they should not die. Tiberinus handed the babies to a she-wolf who lived in a nearby cave. The she-wolf raised the boys as if they were her own cubs, feeding them and protecting them from harm. She was helped by a woodpecker, who brought extra food to feed the boys as they grew into sturdy toddlers.

One day, the twins wandered far away from the cave, away from the protection of the she-wolf and the woodpecker. Soon they found themselves lost and frightened in a dark wood. Their cries drew the attention of an old shepherd named Faustulus. Faustulus was astonished to find two young boys in the wood. He looked carefully at the twins, both of whom looked very much like old King Numitor. He remembered the story of Rhea Silvia's twin sons, who had been left to die on the banks of the River Tiber, and he wondered if these might be the same boys. Faustulus took the twins to his village home, and raised them as his own sons.

Living with Faustulus in his village home, Romulus and Remus learned how to tend the sheep on the hillside. They both became excellent shepherds, but neither wanted to spend their life working with sheep. That was just too dull. The twins were brave and clever and popular; they wanted to live a life of excitement and adventure. Realising that the twins were about to leave him, Faustulus told Romulus and Remus what he had long suspected: that they were the lost twin sons of Rhea Silvia, and the heirs to the throne of their grandfather, King Numitor.

Hearing the story of good King Numitor and his evil brother Amulius for the first time, Romulus and Remus grew very angry. They were determined to teach Amulius a lesson. They would put their grandfather, Numitor, back on the throne of Alba Longa, and release their mother, Rhea Silvia, from her locked room in the palace. Romulus and Remus hugged Faustulus goodbye, and set off for the city of Alba Longa.

All went according to plan. The brothers arrived at the Alba Longa palace, and knocked loudly on the door. They demanded a meeting with King Amulius, and introduced themselves. Amulius was astonished and frightened. He had thought that Rhea Silvia's children were long dead, and now here they both were, standing before him. Romulus and Remus politely asked Amulius to hand the throne back to their grandfather Numitor, but Amulius refused. There was a brief fight, and Amulius was killed. The twins then searched the caves outside the city

walls, until they found Numitor. They brought him back to the palace, gave him a bath, clean clothes and a good meal, and declared him king of Alba Longa once again. Numitor's first deed as king was to release his daughter, Rhea Silvia, from her locked room.

With Numitor back on the throne of Alba Longa, and Rhea Silvia released from her locked room, everyone should have been happy. The people of Alba Longa certainly were. At last they had their beloved King Numitor back again. But Romulus and Remus were restless and dissatisfied. They had been had been clever and brave, and had defeated an evil king. Their grandfather now had his throne and their mother now had her freedom, but they had gained nothing from their great adventure. They decided that they would build their own city, so that they too could rule as kings.

Hugging their mother and grandfather goodbye, Romulus and Remus set off on a quest to find a suitable site to build a new city. This should have been easy, but the twins could not agree. Whenever Romulus liked a particular site; Remus hated it. Whenever Remus liked a particular site: Romulus hated it. Romulus wanted to build on the top of one hill; Remus wanted to build on the top of an entirely different hill. Romulus believed that the gods wanted him to pick the site for the new city; Remus believed that the gods wanted him to pick it. The brothers quarrelled day and night, until finally Romulus had a good idea.

90

"Surely the best place for us to build our new city is on the bank of the River Tiber; at the place where we were abandoned in a basket as babies."

Remus agreed that this was indeed the best plan, and the brothers decided to build their new city on the banks of the River Tiber.

Romulus started to build the new city, but Remus refused to help. He stood watching and laughing as Romulus worked very hard to build a low stone wall around the edge of the new city. Then suddenly, without warning, as Romulus was digging a well to provide water for the new city, Remus jumped over the low wall and pushed Romulus to the ground. With Romulus lying at his feet still clutching his spade, Remus claimed the new city as his own: "I have invaded your city, Romulus, and have defeated you. Now the city is mine. I will name the new city Reme, after me. I will be its king and you will be nothing. You will live in a cave outside the city walls!"

Furious, Romulus leapt to his feet. He rushed at his brother, and hit him with the spade. Remus died instantly. Romulus buried his brother, cried over his grave, and then continued to build. Soon a splendid new city stood on the banks of the River Tiber. Romulus named his new city Rome, after himself.

ABOUT ROMULUS'S STORY

All the other stories in this book come from ancient Greece, but this story comes from ancient Rome. It explains to the Roman people how their city was built by Romulus on the bank of the River Tiber. In fact, the story is a legend, and is not true. But Rome is a real city.

Rome started as a small settlement, but it quickly grew to become the centre of a mighty empire which stretched from northern England to Syria and north Africa (you may need to look these places up on a map) and which ruled many millions of people. Today Rome is the capital city of the modern country called Italy. The people who live in modern Rome speak Italian. The people who lived in ancient Rome spoke a different language, called Latin. Here are some Latin words for you to learn:

Hello:	*salve*
Goodbye:	*vale*
Yes:	*ita vero*
No:	*nullum*
Boy:	*puer*
Girl:	*puella*

WHAT DO YOU THINK?

1. Do you know what a woodpecker is?

2. Who is Faustulus?

3. Why did the twins decide to build their new city on the bank of the River Tiber?

4. Can you find Rome on a map?

PEOPLE AND PLACES

ACRISIUS: the king of Argos and grandfather of Perseus

AEGEUS: the king of Athens and father of Theseus

ALBA LONGA: an ancient Italian city

AMULIUS: an unkind man, king of Alba Longa and great-uncle of Romulus and Remus

APHRODITE: the Greek goddess of love

APOLLO: the Greek sun god, an expert musician

ARACHNE: a big-headed girl who wove beautiful tapestries

ARGOS: a Greek kingdom

ARIADNE: the clever daughter of King Minos of Crete

ARTEMIS: the Greek goddess of hunting

ATALANTA: a brave princess who could run very fast

ATHENA: the Greek goddess of wisdom, an expert weaver

ATHENS: a Greek kingdom

CORINTH: a Greek kingdom

CRETE: an island in the Mediterranean Sea

DAEDALUS: an inventor and architect, the father of Icarus

DANAË: the daughter of Acrisius and mother of Perseus

DEMETER: the Greek goddess of harvest and farming

DIONYSUS: the Greek god of the wine harvest

EPIMETHEUS: the brother of Prometheus and husband of Pandora

EURYALE: one of the three Gorgon sisters

FAUSTULUS: a kind old shepherd who finds Romulus and Remus
    wandering in the wood

GORGONS: three cruel snake-haired sisters whose eyes could turn
    living people into stone

GREY ONES: three very old women who shared one eye and one tooth

HADES: the Greek god who ruled the Underworld

HERMES: the Greek messenger god

HIPPOMENES: a clever young man in love with Atalanta

HOPE: the last creature to escape from Pandora's box

IASOS: the father of Atalanta

ICARUS: the son of Daedalus, who did not listen to his dad

JOCASTA: the queen of Thebes and mother of Oedipus

LABYRINTH: a maze underneath the palace on the island of Crete, home to the Minotaur

LAIUS: the king of Thebes and father of Oedipus

LYDIA: An ancient kingdom in Turkey

MARS: the Roman god of war and farming

MEDUSA: one of the three Gorgon sisters; her head was covered with hissing snakes

MIDAS: a kind but foolish king

MINOS: the king of Crete and master of the Minotaur

MINOTAUR: a creature with the body of a man and the head and horns of a bull, who likes to eat young men and women

MOUNT OLYMPUS: the home of the Greek gods and goddesses

NAIAD: a water spirit

NUMITOR: a good man, the king of Alba Longa and grandfather of Romulus and Remus

OEDIPUS: the son of King Laius and Queen Jocasta of Thebes

PAN: a Greek god and expert in playing the reed pipes

PANDORA: a beautiful girl who disobeyed Zeus, and opened a box

PASIPHAË: the wife of King Minos of Crete

PERSEPHONE: the daughter of Demeter and wife of Hades

PERSEUS: a brave young man who killed the Gorgon

POLYBUS: the king of Corinth who adopts Oedipus

POLYDECTES: the king of Seriphos

PROMETHEUS: the man who stole the secret of fire from the gods

REMUS: the twin brother of Romulus

RHEA SILVIA: the daughter of Numitor and mother of Romulus and Remus

ROME: an ancient Italian city

ROMULUS: the twin brother of Remus

SERIPHOS: an island in the Mediterranean Sea

SICILY: an island in the Mediterranean Sea

SILENUS: an old teacher

SPHINX: a creature with the head of a woman, the body of a lion, the wings of an eagle and the tail of a snake

STHENO: one of the three Gorgon sisters

THEBES: a Greek kingdom

THESEUS: a brave prince, the son of Aegeus, king of Athens

TIBER: the river that flows through Rome

TIBERINUS: the god of the River Tiber

ZEUS: king of the Greek gods and goddesses

ZOË: the daughter of King Midas

WHAT DO YOU THINK? – ANSWERS

1. PERSEPHONE VISITS THE UNDERWORLD

1. Why did the people love Demeter?

The people loved Demeter because she worked very hard to provide them with food. Without her hard work, they would have been very hungry indeed.

2. What does a pomegranate look like?

The pomegranate is a round fruit with a thick red skin. It is roughly the size of an apple. If an adult cuts it open for you, you will see that it is filled with many hundreds of seeds. The Greeks regarded these pomegranate seeds as a great delicacy.

3. Do you know how many months there are in each year? And how many days there are in each month?

There are twelve months in every year. To remember how many days there are in each month, you just need to remember this very old rhyme, which I was taught at school: *Thirty days has September, April, June and November. All the rest have thirty-one, Except February, which has twenty-eight, or twenty-nine in a leap year.*

4. What foods do you think the ancient Greeks ate?

The ancient Greeks loved to eat grains (which they made into bread and cake), vegetables and fruits including olives, grapes, pomegranates, figs, and beans. They kept sheep and goats, which provided them with milk, cheese and meat. Those who lived near the sea also ate a lot of fish and shellfish.

2. PANDORA OPENS A BOX

1. *Where do the gods and goddesses live?*

The gods and goddesses live on Mount Olympus, the highest mountain in Greece. Can you find Mount Olympus on a map?

2. *Who is Zeus?*

Zeus is the king of the gods. His home is on Mount Olympus.

3. *Why do you think that the people wanted the secret of fire?*

The people wanted the secret of fire so that they could have heat and light in their homes. This allowed them to stay warm in winter, to cook food, and to melt metal. It also allowed them to light lamps to see at night.

4. *Why did Pandora open the box?*

Pandora opened the box, even though she had been told not to, because she could not control her curiosity.

3. THESEUS ESCAPES FROM THE LABYRINTH

1. *Can you find the island of Crete on a map? And Athens?*

   Look at the map at the front of this book.

2. *What did the Minotaur look like? You may like to draw him.*

   The Minotaur had the body of a man, but the head and horns of a bull. He also had hairy feet!

3. *Why did Ariadne give Theseus a large ball of wool?*

   Ariadne knew that Theseus would be able to kill the Minotaur with the sword that she gave him. But he would then be lost in the twisting tunnels of the Labyrinth, and he could die of hunger and thirst if he could not find the door. So she told him to tie the end of the ball of wool to the door, and to unwind the wool as he made his way through the tunnels. With the Minotaur dead, he could then easily follow the wool trail back to the door and escape from the Labyrinth.

4. *Why did King Aegeus die?*

   King Aegeus saw the ship returning to Athens from Crete. Because Theseus had forgotten to change the ship's sails from black to white, he assumed that his son had been killed by the Minotaur. He did not want to live if his son was dead, so he threw himself off a cliff, into the sea.

4. ICARUS FLIES NEAR THE SUN

1. Daedalus is an inventor and an architect. Do you know what an architect is?

An architect is a man or woman who designs buildings.

2. Which animal makes wax and honey?

Bees make wax and honey.

3. Why does Icarus fall into the sea?

Icarus falls into the sea because he ignored his Dad's good advice. Daedalus knew that the wax holding Icarus' wings together would melt in the heat of the sun. As Icarus flew higher and higher, his wings started to melt.

4. Can you draw a picture of Icarus and Daedalus flying in the sky?

Well done if you drew a picture.

5. ATALANTA RUNS A RACE

1. *What kind of animal is a boar?*

A boar is a male pig. A female pig is called a sow, and baby pigs are called piglets. Wild boars, like the boar that Artemis sent to destroy the crops and frighten the people, can be very fierce.

2. *Who is the Greek goddess of hunting?*

Artemis is the Greek goddess of hunting.

3. *What prize did Atalanta receive for being the first hunter to wound the huge boar?*

Atalanta was given the boar's skin and head as her prize.

4. *How many golden apples did Hippomenes drop in the race?*

Hippomenes dropped three golden apples in the race.

6. MIDAS IS UNLUCKY

1. *Who is Dionysus?*

Dionysus is the Greek god of the wine harvest.

2. *What is King Midas' daughter called?*

King Midas' daughter is called Zoë. Zoë means "life" in the ancient Greek language.

3. *King Midas wished that everything he touched would turn to gold. Why was that a silly wish?*

It was a silly wish because he needed to be able to touch some things, including people, food and drink, without turning them to gold.

4. *What job does a barber do?*

A barber cuts men's and boys' hair.

7. PERSEUS KILLS A GORGON

1. Who is Hermes?

Hermes is the Greek messenger god. He lends Perseus a pair of winged sandals which will allow him to fly, and a helmet which will allow him to become invisible.

2. What pieces of equipment do the gods and goddesses lend to Perseus?

The goddess Athena lends Perseus a polished metal shield. Zeus, the king of the gods, lends him sharp sword. Hermes, the messenger god, lends Perseus two things; a pair of winged sandals which will allow him to fly, and a helmet that will make him invisible.

3. How many eyes and teeth do the Grey Ones have?

Although there are three Grey Ones, they have only one eye and one tooth between them. They have to share!

4. Medusa has the body of a great slithery serpent, the arms and head of a woman, a large tongue, metal claws and hissing snake-hair. Can you draw her?

Well done if you drew a picture.

8. ARACHNE WEAVES A WEB

1. Who is Athena?

Athena is the Greek goddess of wisdom. She is an expert weaver.

2. Which animal provided Arachne with wool?

Sheep provide Arachne with wool. Wool is the soft, curly hair of a sheep. It is cut off the sheep's body in much the same way that a hairdresser or barber cuts your hair. The cutting of the sheep's wool is called shearing.

3. What equipment does Arachne use to weave her tapestry?

Arachne uses a loom to weave her tapestry. And, of course, she uses wool.

4. Arachne is transformed into a spider. Do you know how many legs a spider has?

A spider always has eight legs. There are more than 45,000 different types of spider in the world!

9. OEDIPUS MEETS THE SPHINX

1. Why did King Laius leave his new baby son under a tree on a mountain in the far-away land of Corinth?

King Laius left his new baby son under a tree on a mountain in the far-away land of Corinth because he was worried that the boy would one day kill him. He thought that if he abandoned the baby, the baby would die.

2. Who killed King Laius?

Oedipus killed King Laius, when they quarrelled on the path to Thebes.

3. The Sphinx is a frightening creature with the head of a woman, the body of a lion, the wings of an eagle and the tail of a snake. Can you draw her?

Well done if you drew a picture.

4. Do you have a favourite joke or riddle? Tell it to your friends or family, and see if you can make everyone laugh.

I hope that everyone laughed really loudly at your joke or riddle. My favourite joke is:

Q: Why do bees have sticky hair?

A: *Because they use honey combs!*

10. ROMULUS BUILDS A CITY

1. Do you know what a woodpecker is?

A woodpecker is a bird with a very strong beak. Woodpeckers usually live near trees, in woods or forests. They use their strong beaks to peck or drum on tree trunks while searching for food, and they also use their beaks to make holes in tree trunks to make their nests. A woodpecker can peck with its beak as many as twenty times in one second. Can you drum your finger on a table twenty times in one second?

2. Who is Faustulus?

Faustulus is a kind an old shepherd who finds Romulus and Remus wandering in the woods, and raises them as his own sons.

3. Why did the twins decide to build their new city on the bank of the River Tiber?

The twins decided to build their new city on the bank of the River Tiber because this was the place where they had been abandoned in a basket as babies.

4. Can you find Rome on a map?

Look at the map at the front of this book if you are struggling to find Rome.